THE SOUND OF LIGHT

Also by John Heath-Stubbs from Carcanet

Sweetapple Earth
Galileo's Salad
Selected Poems

The Literary Essays

JOHN HEATH-STUBBS

THE SOUND OF LIGHT

CARCANET

First published in Great Britain in 1999 by
Carcanet Press Limited
4th Floor, Conavon Court
12-16 Blackfriars Street
Manchester M3 5BQ

Copyright © John Heath-Stubbs 1999

The right of John Heath-Stubbs to be identified
as the author of this work has been asserted
by him in accordance with the Copyright,
Designs and Patents Act of 1988
All rights reserved

A CIP catalogue record for this book
is available from the British Library
ISBN 1 85754 353 X

The publisher acknowledges financial assistance
from the Arts Council of England

Set in 10pt Palatino by Bryan Williamson, Frome
Printed and bound in England by SRP Ltd, Exeter

For Anne, Nick and Maria

Contents

Apple Gripe

They woke as from a drug-induced slumber –
A dream of darkness, of fire that was the darkness,
And in their guts, the gripe of apples.

What had it promised, that sibilant voice,
That affable constrictor? Knowledge –
Knowledge that only gods rejoice in.
They fumbled in the catacombs of their brains
For intimations they'd not known before.
They found mortality – never again
Might they suppose joy would be termless;
They found their nakedness – and sex no longer
Would be uncomplex and without its hate.

Foreclosure of their lease had not
As yet been uttered. That would come, and then,
While Eden withered all about them,
With vagrant lagging steps, they'd take their way
Towards the gate which would be slammed behind them.

The Colour of Sound. The Sound of Light.
For Carlos Klein

Scriabin paused at the piano.
His hands relaxed, but still they lay
On the white and black of the keyboard. Before his eyes
Flashed a vast Indian temple. The colour organ
Swirled red and green and gold. White-robed priests
Swung censers, drifting from them
Exotic and erotic perfumes. All
The orchestral voices sounded and gleamed, with different hues,
While still the trumpet mounted ever upward
Like Promethean flame. So he envisaged
The final consummation –
Man dethrones God at last.

But far remote from this,
In the cold dryness of the sphere of Saturn,
The great contemplatives were dancing,
Just for sheer joy, gyrating
Among the planet's circling rings, about
That Florentine space-traveller Alighieri.

The Brain-Fever Bird

'Brain-fever, brain-fever, brain-fever, brain-fever.'
The monsoon rains still fell, and the bird called
Persistently – created, it would seem
By providence, or possibly Beelzebub,
To plague expatriate Britishers – missionaries,
Medical officers, planters, government officials,
In the remoter jungle stations, till
Their sanity caved in – 'I swear I'll kill that bird.
I'll go into the bush and track it down.'
(Braving presumably, tigers and pythons,
Crocodiles and panthers, at the least
Leeches and ticks.) 'I'll shoot the cursed thing
Before it drives me crazy, sends me cuckoo!'

It was indeed a kind of cuckoo. I suppose
This was its ordinary way to shout
(As Housman put it) all day long at nothing
In soggy jungles, not in leafy dells.

The Empire's finished, but the rains go on,
The bird still sings – and whether now
It says 'Brain-fever' I've no way of knowing –
Other insanity, other rulers here
Its former victims seem to us
Shadowy figures out of Somerset Maugham,
Or out of Rudyard Kipling – but in the heart
There is a rain of blood still falling
For all the madness, waste and cruelty,
Rampaging through the world, and in the skull
A bird unendingly is screaming
'Brain-fever, brain-fever, brain-fever, brain-fever!'

At St Pancras Station

Maybe I've got it wrong, and it's Kings Cross –
But there is a rumour buzzing around that under
One of the departure platforms of
That mighty terminus Sir George Gilbert Scott's
Cathedral to the gods of power and steam,
Lies Boadicea's secret mausoleum –
Fiery-haired Boudicea, Icenian queen.
Her tattooed whooping hordes and ululating
Druid priests, her scything chariots, and her trained war-dogs,
Sacked Colchester and Roman London.
What are those groans and screams you hear at midnight? –
Clanging of brakes, rattle of grinding wheels,
Hiss of vapour – or else the cries
Of those who suffered her atrocities:
Matrons, raped and disembowelled,
Their breasts cut off and stuffed into their mouths,
Sacrifice, and smell of burning flesh
In sacred groves? This is the vengeance
Of all indigenous cultures, scourged, their patrimony stolen
By fiscal fraud and occupying troops –
And this can come again. Commuter standing here,
Awaiting a train for Bedford or from Cambridge,
And cursing Railtrack for a delayed service,
Whisper instead a brief petition
To St Pancras – may he intercede
With all the strength that boy martyr's named for.

Gaetano Donizetti Enters the Mental Hospital

'You are ill, but you will get better,' they said.
They lied, for the spirochaetes
Demolished his brain, ran riot
In the steam of his blood, among the nervous fibres –
'And you will go back to Italy,' they said,
'To Bergamo, to the olive and the vine,
The sunlight, the sound of guitars, and *contadine*
Singing at their labour in the fields.
It's been arranged, and the coach will start tomorrow.'
The coach trotted briskly through the Paris faubourgs,
And then it stopped. 'We have a problem –
The coach has broken down it seems. It will be fixed tomorrow.
Meanwhile – how fortunate – there is this hotel at hand.
We have booked you a room for the night – commodious
    accommodation.
You will have attendance and medical care.'
Was that indeed a hotel –
Standing as it did in its own grounds,
Behind high walls, with windows barred?
As he entered it he heard a door slamming somewhere,
The grinding of a lock, and faint weeping,
And laughter that did not seem hilarious.
But he stayed. It seemed the coach would never start again;
Bleeding and blistering, drugs and potions, a gathering
Of leeches that suckled the back of his head.

Friends came and visited – they must have been friends,
Memory grew dimmer, and faces unfamiliar.
Once he went to the piano and began to play –
They held their breath, was this a sign of recovery?
Only a meaningless succession of discords.
The violence and anguish of another age –
Not yet dreamt of – might explore
Those tonalities, polytonalities,
Atonalities. What other images
Haunted his mind? Images of prison –
Mary Stuart at Fotheringay, the shadow of the block
Growing closer and closer; Anne Boleyn in the tower,
Singing 'Home sweet home' (It was

13

An old English folk song wasn't it?)
And portents of madness –
Lucy Ashton, when they battered down the door,
In her bridal dress bedabbled with blood
And the young man's body, and the stab-wounds:
'Tak' up your bonny bridegroom!'
But favour and prettiness. No nightingale
Twittered so sweetly, nor no tame canary,
Nor captive bullfinch schooled
By a small reed-organ. How the crowd
Had cheered and cheered again – 'Bis! Bis!

Ancora. Viva Donizetti!'
Loudest of all, applauding
In the too extravagant box, her glance
Swivelling between the footlights and the diva,
And the face of her flashy sexually confident lover,
Poor provincial Emma Bovary.

The Young Orestes
(Homage to Jacques Offenbach)

'The Mozart of the Champs Elysées' (and/or his librettist)
In *La Belle Hélène*, I'm sure got it right:
(A soprano *travestie* role of course)
In the whirlpool of puberty – he's accompanied his father
Agamemnon, and his uncle Menelaus,
To the jamboree at Sparta, where his uncle will compete,
With the other chieftains, for the hand of Helen
(Begotten by a chenomorph bird,
A god's disguise). Bubbling away, Orestes can't wait
To explore the night-spots of Sparta – of course there were plenty.
That spoilsport, Lycurgus, the law-giver,
Wouldn't come along for a few centuries.
Orestes' mother, of course, is not of the party –
At last he's got away from her apron-strings. I know
The teenage Orestes was just like that –
Before those disastrous events at Mycenae:
Such things are enough to push
A sensitive and highly-sexed young man
Over the edge, and deliver him
Into the talons of the blood-drooling Erinnyes,
With cobras braided in their horrible hair, to suffer
The whistle and steely swish of their whips. It is a commonplace –
Tragedy and farce are closer than you'd think.

Cinna the Poet
(Julius Caesar, Act 3, Scene 3)

Remember Cinna the poet – in Shakespeare?
Torn to pieces by the mob, because
He happened to bear the same cognomen
As one of Julius Caesar's murderers.

Tough on Cinna the poet – and tougher still –
His verses only survive in a few fragments
Quoted by grammarians to prove a point.
He was one of the neoterics – a greek term
Roughly translated as modernists.

I hope he has a place in that noble castle
Which Dante imagined in limbo – a bit draughty,
The air being always tremulous with sighs –
But at least he can chat with Virgil and with Horace.

Florus and Hadrian
Freely based on some Latin verses

'I'd not be Hadrian, no way I'd be Caesar,
Bitten by gnats, battered by bad weather,
Campaigning on the Germanic frontier,
Against the utmost hordes.'

'I'd not be Florus, Florus the poet,
Blown by bluebottles, poisoned by bad wine,
Doing his rounds of the less respectable
Taverns of Rome, the capital
Of civilisation I've got to fight for.'

If Antonio

If Antonio hadn't picked the right casket, what
Would have happened to Portia, one ventures to wonder.
If she had married the Prince of Morocco
She would, by treaty I suppose,
Have been permitted to practise
Her own faith within his harem,
But there would have been a rumour
That she was making converts among the other women;
As for the treasure he showered upon her
People said that she used it
For the ransom and manumission of Christian captives,
And some went in aid of the Jewish community
(She had a guilty conscience, it seems, about Jews).
There would have been a bow-string prepared for her strangling
Or a sack thrown into the sea
And she in it, if she hadn't sneaked away,
Along with Nerissa, her faithful maid,
The two disguised as boys, and with gold coins and jewels
Sewn up in their underwear, down to the port,
Where, they bribed a sea-captain and chartered a light felucca,
Successfully navigated the straits of Messina
(Nerissa was a gondolier's daughter – didn't you know?)
Turned left up the Adriatic –
Then back to Venice and Belmont again.

But if it had been the foppish Prince of Aragon,
Her intelligence would only have thrown into relief
His utter vapidity. A republican movement,
Not undiscouraged by her began to foment
Among the plebians, until in the end
The Prince was overthrown, and sent into exile,
And the Lady Portia, by unanimous acclaim
Was immediately elected
The first President of their republic.

A Country Minuet

'Old men ought to be explorers.'
The remark, it seems, was Joseph Haydn's.
He often said it in his final years –
Years of *The Creation*, of his last quartets.
Though somebody else was foxy enough –
Or possumish enough – magnificently to annexe it.
And as for me – with a certain element of disbelief –
I have to recognise that I am also
An old man now. And if my words
Cannot join that circling Heraclitan dance –
Earth-dance of East Coker, fire of Little Gidding,
Let them innovate at least the formal steps
Of a country minuet.

Variations on a Popular Song
(A study in banality)

> 'Home, home on the range
> Where the deer and the antelope play;
> Where seldom is heard
> A discouraging word,
> And the skies are not cloudy all day.'

Home, home on the ridge,
Where the bear and the platypus dance;
No way will you find
A thought of some kind –
If you might, you'd be warned in advance.

Home, home in the swamp,
Where leviathan heaves into view –
You may lap, you may drink,
But you'd better not think –
You'll be mulcted, for sure, if you do.

A Fisherman's Tale

I cast my line into the pool – that is,
The unruffled waters of my consciousness –
And wait for the float to bob, then I haul up
A gasping, gleaming, flapping fish – that is,
A poem, but more often these days
An old boot, a broken bottle, discarded sandwich box –
Just a bad joke. Better dispose of it
Into the mud, into the trash basket –
Unless it be a sign
That I am turning, in the end, post-modern.

The Yellow Bird

He read a poem about a painting,
Apologising: 'I know,' he said,
'That's something you're told you never should do.'
'Who was it told you,' I asked him afterwards,
'You shouldn't write a poem about a painting?'
'It's generally said,' he answered. I suspected him
Of being addicted to those conventicles
Commonly known as 'poetry workshops',
Where a minor poet earns an honest crust
Instructing a nestful of half-fledged bardlings.

Wit of the staircase – I ought to have told him
In poetry there are no 'Thou shalt nots' –
Only a much more difficult commandment:
Whatever you do, however marginal, however trivial,
        must seem to you
Potentially better than anything
Anyone else has done before –
Like Paul Klee's yellow bird
Casually perching upside down on a cloud.

Letter to Dannie Abse

I thought you were my friend – I'm certain of it:
For half a century or more we've been so,
And I am yours too – there's no doubt of that.
But what about this article in which
You call me 'John Heath-Stubbs, the blind poet'.
In the sort of way one might mention
'Porkie the learned pig' or 'Hans
The calculating horse'. I am a poet –
Or it's permitted that I hope I am –
Who happens to be blind. That inconvenience
Need not define me just because it was
The self-inflicted wound of Oedipus.
And then comes up that word I hate so much –
'Erudite'. I am not erudite.
I may bring in some fact or another
My readers haven't heard of. I like to tease them,
And they can always look it up, and be
Better instructed for it. They love quiz shows
So why should they hate me? Think of a magpie
Who's stashed away a few white stones,
Purloined a silver spoon or two,
Or else a chaplet of gleaming pearls.
That does not make of him
A monster brooding on his secret hoard –
Fafnir the dragon, Harpagon, Volpone.

At the Dylan Thomas Centre, Swansea

I don't believe it, I bloody well don't believe it –
The man, who, forty years since, I joked and drank with
In scruffy pubs and clubs, is sitting out there –
A hulking great bronze statue, they've made of him,
As he sings in his chains like the sea.

The Chucking-Out Bells of Soho
in the Forties and Fifties

I

Kettles and pans, say the bells of St Anne's –
That was a couplet in the original rhyme
Of the London church bells, appropriate at the time
When it was composed, some three centuries ago –
For ironmongers' shops graced the streets of Soho.
But kettles and pans, and objects of that kind,
Were hardly what we expected to find
When my friends and I were likely to be seen
Walking those streets – Old Compton, Frith and Dean,
And that other area north of Oxford Street
Where Marylebone, Holborn and St Pancras meet,
Which those who didn't know it, nowadays may choose
To call Fitzrovia – a name we didn't use.
Of St Anne's church only the tower still stood,
(Though foundation stone of a new church was latterly laid),
And from its eminence no bell could be heard;
Muriel Belcher's coffee stall abutted the burial yard,
Where Theodore, King of Corsica, lay interred –
And Hazlitt also rested, if you can suppose
That heart, passionate for liberty, could ever find repose.
But pub-bells, chiming and whirring, just at eleven o'clock,
Time, gentlemen, please, gave us a kind of shock.
If, like the old church bells, they'd recited a mellow rhyme,
These are the phrases that might have made up their chime –

II

'Just time for a piss!'
Said the bell of the Swiss.

'Go home with your wench,'
Said the bell of the French,
'Your doxie or tart –
We don't give a fart.'

'Or maybe a boy,'
Said the bell of the Fitzroy.

'Be careful what he might try on!'
Said the bell of the Golden Lion.

'A bit of rough trade
We're too much afraid.'

'Well dressed or well built,'
Said the Highlander in his kilt.

'It'll all end in grief,'
Said the bell of the Wheatsheaf.

'Or a good deal worse!'
Said the bell of the Black Horse.

'Beware of such charms,'
Said the bell of the Bricklayers' Arms.

'So end your smart talk,'
Said the bell of the Duke of York.

'And we'll still wish you luck,'
Said the bell of the Dog and Duck.

'All your nights, all your days!'
Said the bell of Auntie May's.

'You gobblers and goonies,'
Brogued the Irish Bell of Mooney's.

'Or just drop down dead,'
Said the bell of the Old Queen's Head.

III

And so it was we stumbled home,
Through streets still haunted by the ghosts
Of Arthur Rimbaud and of Paul Verlaine,
Likewise the foolish shade of Francis Thompson,
Who had once lurked all day in the Public Bar
Of the Pillars of Hercules; inky fingered, down at heel,
The spectre of Karl Marx still wept
For cruelties his followers even then were perpetrating.
Single or in couples, so they went –
The drinkers – some to coffee bars
Open late nights, or seedy clubs,
Or Lyons' Corner House which never closed.
And others made their way – by bus, by tube,
Or – affluent by taxi or else
A long foot-slog to Notting Hill or Chelsea,
Shepherd's Bush, West Hampstead, or wherever,
To cheerless bedsits, or damp basement flats,
Or draughty attic rooms – those for whom the bars
In a real sense were home – the only places
Where, for a few short hours,
They could relate to other human beings.

An East-End Romance

A young adolescent from Hackney
Loved a pretty greek girl called Arachne
He took her to dances
But she spurned his advances
On account of his terrible acne.

That charming greek girl called Arachne,
Repelled by the teenager's acne,
Went to lectures at nights
Upon spiders and mites,
Aimed to educate adults in Hackney.

That unhappy young fellow from Hackney
Was to suffer life-long with his acne,
Although he took lots
Of things for his spots –
But he never forgot sweet Arachne.

A Ballad of Trafalgar Square

Good Lord Nelson stands up there,
Caressed by London's polluted air,
Presiding over Trafalgar Square.

The starlings and pigeons fluttering by
Spit in his one available eye
Or sometimes alight at his feet and die.

'It's lonely on watch here,' Nelson said,
'Please don't send me the wife I wed,
But Emma, so sweet, so accomplished in bed.'

But Landseer's sculptured lions said, 'We
Are symbols of British propriety,
Set here to keep off such trollops as she.'

Nurse Cavell, round the corner, said, 'Stuff!'
(Angel of mercy – but she was tough.)
'Patriotism is not enough –

'A man needs company, that's quite clear.'
'That vacant pedestal in the Square –
His Cheshire chitterling could have been there,'

Said that other lion, upon the façade
Of St Martin's church, as he joined the tirade
In a roaring leonine rhodomontade.

'Nobody needs to be quite forlorn –
Myself have a mate, with a rampant horn –
Though he's only a mythical unicorn.'

Madame Blavatsky in Oxford

Madame Blavatsky – let us not quibble –
Outrageous charlatan, or Theosophic sibil –
Visiting Oxford (this tradition
Comes down it seems by oral transmission)
Formed an acquaintance, even an alliance,
With the eminent professor of natural science.
Some experiments she said, she wanted to do
In a suitable location, where she knew
She wouldn't be disturbed, so could she please
Use his laboratory, and borrow the keys.
With a slight reservation he gave his consent,
But wondered what sort of experiment
This ridiculous woman might be carrying out;
And finally, troubled by a nagging doubt,
He let himself in to the lab one morning,
Using his own keys, but without warning.
He was deeply shocked by what he then saw –
A plain violation of natural law.
He really believed he was going dafters –
For up there floating about in the rafters
Like an inflated rubber balloon
(A sight which made him ready to swoon)
Was that enormous Russian woman.
The poor professor was only human –
Sickened with indignation, and more
He threw up and vomited all over the floor.
'You wicked creature,' he halloed out clear,
'You horrible bitch come down from there.
Return me my keys – and I'll make it plain
You shall never be let in here again!'
She slowly floated down. With a shout
He grabbed his keys and he chucked her out.
And like an ill-remembered dream
She departed the groves of Academe.

Yogic Flying

Our mystical guru from Katmandu
(Although a decidedly fat man too)
In all kinds of weather
Could float like a feather
Or fly through the air like old Batman do.

The Dandelion and the Daisy, a Fable
For John Fitton

An acrid, milky dandelion,
Gold coroneted, claimed, forsooth,
Descent from an old Norman scion –
From the bold knight, Sir Lion-tooth,
Yet loved an innocent little daisy,
And wooed her with an ardent passion –
Feelings that nearly drove him crazy –
But she just answered in this fashion:
'Time, he passes with a puff,
As golden turn to hoary locks –
And you will learn it soon enough
When kids play dandelion-clocks;
My petals close when light has fled –
So just shut up old Piss-a-bed!'

Senecio

'You can't move anywhere in England these days,' remarked
    Senecio,
'Without treading upon a university.'
Senecio was, of course, an Oxford man.
'Don't talk to me of progress.' He added:
'Ever since I can remember
We've had practically nothing else –
And a nice mess it's got us into.'

Guardian angels tidied up Senecio,
Inserting his soul into a ragwort plant
(His botanical namesake). Magnificent
Scarlet and black day-flying moths
Frequented the golden blaze of his flowers –
But if cattle browsed on the rank leaves,
Their udders were filled with blood as well as milk.

Before all this progress business started
Senecio so much disliked, such a phenomenon
Might have led to an eccentric belle dame
In a nearby cottage, being thrown in the horsepond,
Hauled out if she floated, charged with witchcraft,
Sent up to the sessions, tried, found guilty,
And hanged by the neck until she was damned well dead.

There's something to be said for progress, after all,
Though it has its drawbacks, one must admit.

Hansel and Gretel

The forms of the names, I think, are South German.
It is a tale I find disturbing, in spite
Of Humperdinck's lumpish folk-tunes.
There were hard times still in the peasant memory
When children were driven out into the forest
To fend for themselves. Their parents loved them
But for all that, half-hoped they wouldn't come back.
Too many witches have been pushed into ovens,
Incinerated, as enlightened centuries later
Were Jews and Gypsies. Children were turned
Not into gingerbread but bars of soap.

There is no sandman, no fairy of the dew
Nor, Engelbert, a flight of tinselled angels
Descending to keep watch
Over the sleep of innocents: nor, when past bearing
Our grief becomes, will Heaven send its succour.

Note: The witch persecutions of the seventeenth century
were at their worst in South Germany and Austria.

To a Photographer on his Fiftieth Birthday

'The wickedest invention of the modern age.'
It was Wystan Auden pontificated thus;
Elizabeth Barrett surely was wiser
When she heard about this new-found process –
'Just think of having the shadow of someone you love
To keep forever.'

But for you it's all in a flash – a flash of insight –
Encompassing perhaps the soul
Of an Irish town, or the gaunt figure
Of Samuel Beckett holding in his hand
A volume of Leopardi's poems
(Leopardi had looked
Into the same void), or myself
Tall and grey in the Rollright Stones.

At this middle point – what can I wish you?
May the flashes of insight, the flicker of shadows continue;
And the generosity of ale, and wine, and whisky.
The benediction of birdsong at nightfall, and with it
That of the dead, who lie at peace
In the burial ground you live alongside.

Ten Kinds of Birds
For John Minihan

Ten different kinds of birds I have identified
By their calls and songs as we sit here
Under a darkening sky of June, drinking our wine.
It was the wheezing call of the greenfinch
Greeted me on my arrival;
The robin redbreast, that sang to us
All the long Winter through, is hardly trying now –
I guess his brood is fledged and flown; from a fruit-tree
    near the house
The unpretentious song
Of the garden-warbler comes; the sparrow
Has only got one note, but he's working on it.
More eloquent the blackbird – there are two blackbirds
With adjoining territories – one answers
But not identically, the other's phrases –
Sweet and rich their songs. More shrill, more passionate,
A little way off, a thrush is singing also;
Farther still, perhaps at a copse's edge,
The foolish croodling of the wood-pigeon.

From the church tower, from time to time,
A party of jackdaws flies. They cruise round for a bit,
And then return. They talk to each other,
As is their custom: 'Let's keep together boys –
If there should happen to be a hawk around
She'd likely pick off a straggler.'
Now the not quite English accents
Of the collared dove sound somewhere to the right.
It seems he woke a chaffinch up,
Who then repeated his rattling tattle,
Ending with a phrase that sounds like 'ginger beer'
And then fell silent. So it goes on and on
Till one by one sleep claims the birds
As it must soon claim us. As we go in
There is a last blackbird. With sombre plumes
And golden mouth, he flings his melody
Into the darkness –
So let it be with me, when the night comes.

The Conversation at Pisa

When Giacomo Leopardi arrived at Pisa
They told him, or might have told him,
Two Englishmen, two English poets,
Had lately been there, but they'd left
Some ten days since – exiles from their country
By reason of marital scandals, and, as well,
Anti-establishment political opinions.
They were Byron of course – Milord Byron – and Percy Shelley,
Renegade heir of a Sussex baronet.
And so, by a sheer fluke, he never met them,
To make up a third – three atheists, men said –
(But thinking of Byron's Aberdonian boyhood,
With John Knox's God a wee-Willy-Winkie bogle,
We might say two and a half) –
A triad of free spirits:
Byron with his worldly wisdom, and adolescent pose
Of Cain or Lucifer, his satirical bite,
His tempestuous hatred of all injustice:
Shelley with his head full of Plato and Newton,
Godwin and necessity – necessity of revolution,
The golden years' return, the world's great age renewed;
And the impoverished Italian count,
With his spinal curvature, and his weak eyesight,
Dressed in black like a priest might dress.
He had looked into the illimitable emptiness of all things, and
     had witnessed
The final setting of the moon, the dissolution of harmony,
Sappho cursing love, and Brutus virtue –
And man on a small sandgrain in the vastness of space.
I like to think what talk there might have been
If they indeed had met some evening,
While all the bright and distant stars came out
In the deep Italian sky, and the fireflies danced
Overhead, like poems in the darkness of our world,
And some way off the asiola gave its plaintive cry.

Geoffrey Chaucer in Tuscany

It was no holiday break for him –
That customs official, court hanger-on,
And spare-time poet. He was on a trade mission,
Sent by Edward the Third's government
To the Italian city republics – English coal,
Salted herrings, leather, woollens
For Italian wine and olive oil,
And imported luxury goods – furs from the Black Sea ports,
Spices and sugar and dried raisins
From the Middle East. I guess he drove
A shrewd but fair exchange. But, coming back,
He had the works of Dante Alighieri,
Petrarch, and Boccaccio in his baggage –
And English poetry joined the mainstream.

To the Oriole
(Marciana di Castella)
September 1996

I recognise the call, as you fly,
And a friend confirms
The bright yellow flashing bird. The world knows
That I am blind. The world can never know
What stock of images my inner eye is stored with.
You and your greenish mate I recall
From boyhood books – a golden bird,
A magical bird, not to be encountered,
Save by a fluke beyond my expectations
In woods and fields of our dull Hampshire.
It was in Crete that I was to hear that call,
Ringing down over the treeless
Stony landscape; and again in Italy,
In the Sabine hills, among the holme-oaks
That overhang the Bandusian spring,
Where I with my companions
Honoured the shade of Horace.
When I hear that voice
I know I am in the South – there are walnut trees,
And olive groves and vineyards,
And I feel the sun on my skin. So may the lout
Who's pot-shooting now in the next field,
Spare you. And when Spring comes
Your pendant nest be safe.

Alpine Swifts at Chamonix

It is early evening. The town is *en fête*, it seems –
Togged up in their best, folk stroll in the street.
I sit here with my drink where, a century or more ago
And maybe nearby, sat poor tormented
John Addington Symonds (a sad poet from Clifton,
And a Balliol scholar – the Alpine air
Was balm to his weak lungs). He dreamed
Of a Greece that never really was, and lusted
After young mountain men as they walked past.

There is a shrillness in the air – of swifts –
Not the black screamers that sweep
Over English cities, but Alpine swifts –
White-breasted, with almost translucent wings,
Their home the snowy terraces of Mont Blanc.
Swifts are creation's paragon of birds,
That never touch the ground, that sleep
Upon rising thermals. A bell is tolling
From the church tower for solemn vespers –
What feast is it comes round? Not yet –
St Michael and all angels.

Rafflesia

A parasitic plant, it has
Nor stem, nor leaves. Its rootlets
Infiltrate the trunks of trees, sapping their vital force.
In season it produces one huge flower
Which looks and smells like rotten meat. Flies
Attempt to lay their eggs there, and that way
Unwittingly cross-pollinate. It is a jungle wonder,
That honours the name of the great enlightened
Sir Stamford Raffles, founder of Singapore
(Not the gentleman cracksman). God
Has made all things well.

Rotifer

In a small pool of water, or among damp moss,
The little rotifer sits, anchored by a stem
Continually sweeping into its mouth
Even more microscopic particles of food,
By a tiny circle of swirling hairs
That look like a wheel. Sometimes, indeed,
It disengages itself, and wanders about
With a leech-like motion, tail to head.
It has a brain, or a neural ganglion,
Larger in proportion than that of a man
Or any other animal. What does it think of?
Perhaps it ponders transcendental verities
That only the angels ('Macrobes'
As C.S. Lewis called them) delight to contemplate
As they wheel in their ninefold choirs.

Basilisk

The basilisk-lizard of India skitters
Across the stream, supported
By surface tension only. One speed alone –
No more, no less – can make this possible. An awful lot of lizards
Had to drown, before
This adaptation could evolve. Just like
His mythical prototype, he casts
A petrifying eye on the Beagle's surgeon –
Pierces a heart already turned to stone,
Cleansed of faith, God, deprived of poetry –
Darwin, a good and conscientious man,
Whose surgeon's scalpel hangs by Ockham's razor.

The beagle is a dog for country sport.
By artificial selection it is bred
To chase the timid hare, the mad March hare –
And still the intellectual hunt goes on.

Uncle Jim

In the semi-educational books of my boyhood
It was always Uncle Jim who took the children
To the zoo, or to the natural history museum.
He instructed them in the principles of taxonomy:
'The lion, children, belongs to the cat family
But the wolf and the fox are related to the dog.
The hippo is a cousin of the pig
But the rhino is not. He has three front toes –
Not two or four. The whale is not a fish,
The spider is not an insect, and the bat, of course, is not a bird.'
In the BBC schools broadcast he was the Observer
With an imaginary time machine to go to the past:
'Shin up this tree-fern children, we are being chased
By a tyrannosaur – but oh, look –
An archaeopteryx is incubating her eggs
Among the fronds.' Unmarried
Clearly, he was queer as a coot, or gay as a gargany
If not a raging paedophile. No resonances then
Of a house of horrors demolished brick by brick,
Of children tortured and starved in the cellerage
Their whitening bones beneath the floorboards.
But a nurturing pattern,
Through the weft and warp of the animal kingdom –
Wild ganders loyally mated for life,
Damon and Pythias as youthful giraffes,
Adolescent crushes between bull-elephants;
Fabre observed it even among his insects.

The Amphisboena

The amphisboena – not a snake,
Nor yet perhaps a lizard, nor anything at all
Except an amphisboena – he can move back and forth
His head and tail being virtually indistinguishable.
Alarmed, he sometimes waves his tail about,
Just as a striking cobra might
Its hooded head. And by this strategy,
If someone tries to hit him with a stick,
Old Amph can make a getaway –
His head uninjured, though his tail be battered.

My poems, I sometimes think
Are rather like the anomalous amphisboena –
For no one can make head or tail of them.

Dialogue of Bees

Deborah and Melissa, two honey-bees,
Golden amazons, virgins armed
With a poisoned dirk, ranged over the fields
Of bean-flowers, oil-seed rape,
Buttercup meadows, and incense-breathing gorse,
Gathering nectar and granules of pollen.
They conversed together as they flew –
In their dancing language, with entrechats and pirouettes
For verbs and for adverbs. Sweet Melissa
Said to her friend, 'Has it ever occurred to you? –
Those hulking creatures called human beings
Wave their front limbs about, open their mouths
Emitting air in possibly significant patterns –
Might it be feasible, that they possess
A kind of intelligence, even a language?'
The sensible Deborah made reply:
'Such speculations only distract
From our social destiny – to serve the Hive
And its Holy Matriarch. Let us put our trust
In the Ineffable Hum or Om,
The great Hexapod in the sky.'

The Crab Spiders' Wedding

'One thing I must make clear –' said the female crab spider,
'After those nuptial ecstasies we're about to embark on
You'll be nothing more to me than a quick intake
Of a high-grade protein. I shall need it
To give those several hundred offspring you're about to beget
A proper start in life.' 'The point is taken,'
Said the male crab spider, 'And well put too,
But while you were putting it you failed to notice
That I had tied you down with a silken thread –
The web which all our tribe can spin.
But after I've done I promise I'll release you
With a quick snip. And then I'll be off
With a fast getaway, before you've even observed it.
It's true that our offspring may be a bit disadvantaged
From lack of protein – but I'll have plenty of others
By further partners, whom I'll be deeply in love with,
And tie up too, in exactly
The self-same way as you, my darling.'

Poem for the End of the World

Some day, it seems, the cosmos will,
Turning impatient, throw a planet at us,
Or else a filthy snowball of a comet;
Or we will stifle in our effluent –
That sort of thing, we're told,
Put paid to the dinosaurs – lumbering Diplodocus,
Leggy Iguanodon, baroque Triceratops, or Stegosaur,
Tyrannosaurus with his dagger thumbs –
Pals of our childhood,
Or of the earth's childhood – that will be
The ultimate news from nowhere
For us, and all our clever progeny:
Our robots and our androids, smart computers.

Some find it reassuring to suppose
An elvish folk will land, as green as tree-frogs,
In delicate porcelain flying saucers, brimming
With lapsang fuchon – Peter Pan
Or Noddy at their head, faster than light
Out of space, or from
The hollow ringing centre of the earth.
Lob-lie-by-the-fire will tidy up our muddle –
It is his métier.

But I recall that northern myth which told
After the final twilight, Baldr returns
With his companions, beautiful
And disremembered deities
That had died once and been forgotten –
And in the scorched grass they will find again
The golden chessmen they had played with once,
The dice which God had cast
Before the first creation of the world.

A Romantic Adventure

Jabez took a package holiday
On a specially constructed satellite
Circling Calisto, which circles Jupiter,
But he was kidnapped by a desperate gang
Of one-armed bandits. The crime was master-minded
By a rogue computer, rotten with viruses
And eaten up with malice too, against
Its own creator, Man (some men hate God
In just that sort of way). Not being a clone,
Jabez had no identicals who could stump up
The money for his ransom; and might
Have perished miserably, had not
A sweet melodious jukebox fallen for him,
Purloined the jailer's keys, and set him free
(The jailer was a large humanoid cockroach).
Then both of them, by way of the internet,
Went back to dull old earth, and lived together,
In perfect harmony, for many years until
Rust consumed her, mortality claimed him.

A Toby Jug
For Robert and Sue

It was near Southend I was shown a shop
Entirely stocked with Toby jugs –
Modern ones of course, of various sizes,
With bright colours painted on the porcelain.
Now I'm a sucker for kitsch of that sort
(I nearly used the ghastly phrase 'Of that ilk')
And so a friend gave me one. I took it home.
Large and flamboyant, he seemed to tower
Over my other bric-a-brac, therefore
I put him away in the kitchen, behind the teapot.
But after a bit, I found a use for him –
To pour custard, tinned custard at that,
Over steamed roly-poly or apple tart.
Humiliating, perhaps you'd think, for poor old Toby
With his eighteenth-century buccaneer persona:
He ought to hold rum or whisky, but nowadays
These come in glass bottles, and I don't decant them;
But Toby's not the only one, of course,
In this nineteen-nineties England of ours
Who has to do a job he wasn't designed for.

The Visiting Angel

'I've brought a poem for you,' said the angel,
Alighting by the table which I write on.
'You can transcribe it in your own manner
(Here's a quill from my wing to do this with).
Translate it from the celestial dialect,
Accommodate to human understanding.
You can put your own signature underneath it
And send it off to an editor – I don't mind.
But I must go now – a lot of us,
An infinite number in fact, are summoned to attend
A dance upon a needle's point – that identical needle
At whose other end rich men and camels
Slip into Heaven, passing through its eye –
Disencumbered of their baggage. Poets
Have baggage too and sometimes do the same.'
Having said that, with a rustle of plumes
The rara avis took off.

Sonnet

For the Spring Dinner of The Omar Khayyam Club, 1996

More than eight hundred years make up the time
(But we can give or take the odd decade)
Since Omar, seated in an arboured shade,
Lifted his glass and saw the young moon climb
The vernal heavens. He, who had measured out
With algebraic skill the vaulted sky,
Where binary Algol winks its Gorgon eye,
Had found no answers to assuage his doubt –
Save what the grape might teach. The wrangling schools –
He heard their arguments but let them pass:
A tot too low, all such chop-logic fools.
For Omar, and for others, who, alas,
Leave vacant places, we, by joyous rules
Of fellowship, invert a well drained glass.

Fitz and the Mouse

'Don't kill that mouse,' said Edward Fitzgerald
To the boy who read to him, being the original
Old man in a dry month etcetera.
'There's room in the universe for all three of us.'

To the Dormouse
which caused the fire in Peter Russell's attic

'Oh Diamond, Diamond,' Newton sighed
When the damage was descried,
'Thou little know'st what thou hast done!'
Diamond his dog, in doggish fun
Scampering about, had overturned
A candle – Newton's notes were burned.
Sir Isaac had to do again
All that work, with tedious pain,
That the enlightened world might learn
By what laws the planets turn
Wheeling in their silent round, and how
Apples tumble from the bough.

For like havoc, Nemesis
Should pursue you, dormouse Glis.
It was you bit through the wire,
Setting Peter's loft on fire.
Manuscripts from famous names
Turned to ashes in the flames;
Letters from Pound and Eliot –
Hungry fire consumed the lot.
So, what retribution's due
To wicked rodents such as you –
Steeped (you wouldn't find it funny)
In genuine Hymettus honey
To please a Roman epicure –
That's the least you should endure!
But we'll forgive you – wander free
Through fields and woods of Tuscany,
Gathering there what they afford:
Nuts to stock your secret hoard,
With stones of apricots and plums.
We all must work – for Winter comes.

Hurrah for Pachyderms

The aardvark and the golden mole
And the two kinds of elephants,
The dugong and the manatee
And hyrax are the sole extant
Survivors of their tribe. The term
We use for it is 'Pachyderm'.

Each one has his special boast –
As with all families of gentry,
Although the aardvark's unaware
His is the OED's first entry –
A kind of honour in its way:
'Hurrah for pachyderms!' I say.

The Giant Squirrels
A Micmac legend

That year giant squirrels came down from the mountains,
Nine feet tall with bushy tails
And prehensile forepaws. They just sat there
And started to eat our bark tepees.
There was nothing much we could do about it.
It was many years later the white men came
With firearms and horses and strange diseases,
And strange beliefs – or no beliefs whatever.
The megatheria on the whole were easier to cope with.

A Clutch of Dinosaur's Eggs
To John Newell

You won't find me much now in bars,
Public or saloon. Put it down if you like
To my age and infirmity – but mostly it's the piped muzak
Drives me out, or even worse
The live music, raucously amplified.

In this double-u-two conurb I've lived in since the sixties
The Duke of Clarence is the house I've favoured –
At least they lay on a decent lunch.

The local dinosaur society (a teenage group)
Has put it about that there is a clutch
Of unhatched dinosaur's eggs under the foundations –
And Dimpna, the Irish barmaid, a simple girl
Lately over from Donegal,
Won't go down there for cellar duty –
There is no way she will.
But as things are now, I'd not be astonished
If an Iguanodon came stomping through the grove,
Following the course of that lost river
Of which we're west of the bourne,
Or a mososaur floundered in the public baths,
Or on the topmost tip
Of St Matthew's a pterodactyl perched.

Variation on a Theme by Tom Moore

That chap in the song, who paces up and down
The empty banquet hall, long after the party
Is finished – candles that blazed
So brightly and so sweetly, are snuffed out now, or else
Their wax has dribbled on the soiled table-cloth
The wreaths have disengaged themselves
From the picture-frames, or where they were tacked to the wall.
Wilted rose-petals make the floor slippery, and out of them
Come little beetles, to be trodden into the carpet.
His thirst for life unquenched, casually
He drinks up somebody else's heel-tap, or nibbles
At a broken cheese-straw, or an after-eight mint.

'. . . ere slumber's chain has bound . . .'
That tune bumbles in my brain like a bee in a bottle –
The stilly night, the stilly night, the chill, chill night.

Goose Flesh

Somewhere or other (it's inevitable)
There is a piece of ground, a cemetery plot,
Wherein one day your bones will lie
(The larval flies, and beetle grubs,
Having feasted, and consummated
Their pre-ordained and honourable task)
Or, maybe, where your ashes will be scattered
By mourning friends – for they'll recall
This was a place that you had loved in life.
But if a goose, a great white portly gaggler,
Or wild grey-lag, barnacle or brent,
Deeming the grass grows greener on that patch,
Breaks ranks, and leaves her sisters,
To waddle over it – that is no reason
Your skin raise pimples now, or your flesh creep.

November
(Derived from Giosue Carducci)

November, evening – fingers of the rain
Tap at the window glass, or is it
My lost companions calling me out
Into the darkness? Patience, friends.
It won't be long now, and I'll not delay.

For the Millennium

Dionysius Exiguus – Dennis the midget
That's what his name means – please don't fidget.
By dint of chronological computation
Worked out the date of the Incarnation –
A task well done. We'll shed no tears
If he got it wrong by about four years:
It's rather more comfortable now that we
Can label centuries AD or BC.
For Time is a monster who devours his progeny –
Kronos or Chronos – see Hesiod's *Theogony*
(A poem that recounts the birth of the gods
Who had to contend against such like odds).
This system robs time of some of its menace –
We ought to be grateful to exiguous Dennis.
It's entirely appropriate that the powers that be,
For the new millennium should now decree
A stately pleasure dome, all made of plastic –
Of course we must all be enthusiastic.
Shall it be a monument to the galloping years? –
Then raise your charged glasses boys, and 'Cheers!'
But for Yeats, a moonlit or a starlit dome
Was an image of eternity – who goes home?

Not Actaeon

Not Actaeon but Artemis
Pursued by tripe hounds which her own flesh bred.

31st August 1997

News from Turcmania

The Turcomans, now that they're free
From Soviet socialist tyranny,
In the main square of every town
Pull effigies of Lenin down,
And then erect, to take their place,
That much-loved hero of their race,
Tamburlaine, the Scourge of God.
I find it all a trifle odd –
Far too much expense and trouble
To grind old Ilyitch down to rubble.
For sure, if my advice they heeded,
A change of make-up's all that's needed.

Mothers of Great Men

'If only Karl would earn some capital,
Instead of just writing about it,'
The mother of Marx is reported to have said.

The son of Madame Buonaparte
Did gain some capital of course –
Doling out kingdoms to his relations.
The money he sent her she prudently stashed away;
'You'll be glad of it one day,' she said,
'When all this nonsense is over.'

Joseph Stalin leaned his head down low,
To catch the words of his dying mother.
'What a pity it is,' softly she whispered,
'You never became a priest, my son.'

The Great God Pan

The great God Pan started being quite a nuisance
In English literature, about the turn
Of the nineteenth-twentieth centuries –
He shows up, remember, in E.M. Forster,
In Saki, and also *The Wind in the Willows* –
But his most tiresome avatar was Peter Pan,
The youthful ruler of the *limbo infantum*
(What else is this world of the Lost Boys –
Condemned to an infantile eternity?).
Peter would fall in love with a succession of Wendies
Who will grow up and marry, turn matronly and forget him –
In his small, pre-pubic corner of hell.
Poor old Barrie, forced as a child
To impersonate a brother who had died,
In order to appease his ferocious mother.
His delicious whimsy delighted the bourgeois –
Darwin had shown how sanguinary nature was, Marx
How piratical were the capitalist classes:
Captain Hook and Mr Darling were one and the same;
Inside the belly of a phallic crocodile –
Freud had stripped its innocence from childhood.

Barrie wrote other plays of course – *Mary Rose*
A delightful study in *dementia praecox*,
Likewise *The Admirable Crichton*,
A charming blueprint for fascism.
But Peter was the icon that would stay with us –
Ritually performed at every Yuletide, while
An alien star is gleaming down
On an unvisited manger, where
The actual Lord of all things
'Has kindly come to dwell in them below'.

The Winter Birds

Birds gathered round the manger, some scraps and crumbs might be
Scattered about in that place of poverty

From the interstellar spaces echoes still rang –
Though few were able to hear it – of the angelic song

Sung to the destitute and the outcast – their story
'Peace down there upon earth, to the high God glory'.

The birds lifted their voices, seeking to augment
Those celestial anthems, each according to his bent.

'As always, as always, my theme is love.'
Soft crooned the voice of the silly ring-dove.

With charcoal feathers the black crow spoke:
'No song you'll get from me – I can only croak.

You want to know the reason? It is because
There is no God, nor will be, nor ever was.'

Then his parti-coloured cousin, the thieving magpie
Uttered her dry laughter in mirthless levity.

A frivolous semi-believer, she'd only don
Half-mourning on the day of the crucifixion.

But the robin in the holly bush, a small brown bird
(Through all the day of cold his sub-song had been heard)

Piped from a breast that would be stained with blood
When he tried to shift the thorns from the crucified saviour's head.

But the mistletoe-thrush, herald of the coming year
With that secret hope of which old Hardy was unaware
Flung his shrill challenge into the turbulent air.

Ockham's Razor

'Categories are not without necessity to be multiplied.'
So said the irrefragible doctor, William of Ockham,
While softly under his breath he muttered, 'That'll knock 'em' –
And well he might, what more was there to say –
As the traditional certainties melted away;
Faith had to make its tremendous leap in the dark.
He's buried in Germany under a car-park.

St Martin's Day

Difficult for St Martin, one might think –
His festival, November the eleventh, in these times
Seems completely swamped by Armistice Day –
That dreary commemoration of guilt and slaughter,
I've always hated from boyhood
But a great day in the middle ages –
The hinder end of harvest – the cattle fattened
On the new-garnered grain, were butchered
(Not enough provender to keep them through the Winter
In that pre-turnip age, but a few kept for stock).
The bones were burned – bone-fires, or bonfires,
Later transferred to November the fifth.
The salted-down meat might last through the Winter,
But when Christmas came on, perhaps a little high –
Better spiced and mingled with raisins,
Coffined in pastry for the festive season –
But St Martin of course can still fix us
A short burst of sunshine before November fogs
Muck up the skies – Martinmas –
A split mantle to keep us from the cold.

Poem for St Bridget's Day
(1 February)
For Mary Montague

In Ireland, I'm told, it's the first day of spring.
That seems optimistic – not even
Mediterranean St Valentine has convened
The birds to their spousals. Only the robin sings,
And the misselthrush, who's feasting
Upon the dead-white, viscous berries
The Druid sickle spared at the Winter solstice.
May St Bridget be kind
To cattle in the shippen. Let them know
They'll soon be out in the open fields again,
Skies are dour and dank – may Heaven send down
One beam at least of solid golden sunshine –
Solid enough for her to hang her cloak on.

Saint Anthony Preaches to the Fishes
(A hint from the German)

Saint Anthony preached to the fishes –
It was an obvious thing to do.
His master, Saint Francis, had preached to the birds
With some success. But they
Were a soft option, for anyhow
They praised the Lord with their songs, and they loved –
At least they loved their mates and their tender brood.
But the fishes, we're told, just went on behaving
Exactly as before, in their cold-blooded
Cannibalistic promiscuous sort of way.
Just one of them swam back for a blessing –
The golden-scaled, pouting-jawed John Dory,
The only fish I think with a Christian name –
I'm glad to have met him, this evening on my plate.

Saint Christopher or Anubis

Giant with a dog's head – a Coptic tradition –
He strides across the dark river. On his shoulders
He carries a child – perhaps
The master of the ford, or just a soul
New-born to Death's obscure kingdom.

Anubis, the jackal-headed god,
Haunter of boneyards, where the scraps
Were cast away of those too poor
For the expensive process of mummification
A spurious immortality. Rich fools
These days rely upon
Crionics, or on cloning.

And I have seen Anubis – or at least
His stone statue, dressed as a Roman soldier,
With his drawn sword, and his stylish helmet
(Commercial art) in the Alexandrian catacombs,
Laid out, some time in Anno Domini
By a speculative mortician – row on row
Of empty sarcophagi, and a space
For eating ritual meals with the dead –
Modern Egyptians still do this (although unsanctioned
By Moslem custom) feasting with the stone guest.

But in those catacombs no one got buried –
No one at all (bad omens perhaps
From the adverse stars). Except in the end
Caracalla's favourite chariot horses –
The emperor who (scandalously) fought
In the public arena, named
For the short gladiatorial cloak he liked to wear
Instead of the formal toga.

We need a psychopomp upon that final road.
A small medallion of St Christopher
Dangles from the ignition keys
Of a Ford Escort which some latter Caracalla
Precipitously drives down the M1, spitting
Death and pollution to the English fields.

A Poem of Welcome

*To the Lord Mayor of Westminster, on the occasion
of his visit to St Matthew's church, Bayswater
(7 December 1997)*

This day let joyful honours crown –
Past Bæga's pool in Pæda's town,
We welcome you to what was once
(Said William Blake, who was no dunce)
A mournful, ever-weeping place –
Paddington, in her disgrace.
She mourned by Tyburn's stream, no doubt,
Where Macheath's gang once prowled about,
Relieving coaches of their load
That trundled down the Oxford road,
Looking for gamesters they might fleece
(In those days there were no police);
For Paddington, they say, was then
A haunt of dangerous desperate men –
A manor of the abbey church
Who sometimes left her in the lurch.
Such things we need not fear nor pity
Now she's incorporate in your city
(Junkies and drabs we have instead,
And those with no roof for their head).
West of the bourne we welcome you
Into this house, where thanks are due
For Matthew at receipt of custom
('A publican, I'll never trust 'em!'
Some said in those days – and in truth
Corruption might infect the booth.)
'Money's the life-blood of the poor.'
And Lazarus lies at Dives' door.
Yet we should know that love of pelf
Is evil's root, not money itself.
A medium of exchange it is
Within the City's arteries.

71

Matthew at his toll-booth heard
The urgent calling of the word.
He rose – he found a second birth,
And wrote down for the whole wide earth,
Instead of charges, rates and dues,
The Master's sayings – joyful news.